Lise Meitner and the Atomic Age

John Bankston

PO Box 196 • Hockessin, Delaware 19707
www.mitchelllane.com

Unlocking the Secrets of Science

Profiling 20th Century Achievers in Science, Medicine, and Technology

Lise Meitner and the Atomic Age

Printing   1   2   3   4   5   6   7   8   9   10

Library of Congress Cataloging-in-Publication Data
Bankston, John, 1974-
    Lise Meitner and the Atomic Age/John Bankston.
        p. cm. —(Unlocking the secrets of science)
    Summary: A biography of the twentieth-century Austrian scientist who, despite facing discrimination as a Jew and a female, made discoveries in nuclear physics which played a major part in the development of atomic energy.
    Includes bibliographical references and index.
    ISBN 1-58415-206-0 (lib. bdg.)
    1. Meitner, Lise, 1878-1968—Juvenile literature. 2. Physicists—Germany—Biography—Juvenile literature. 3. Women physicists—Germany—Biography—Juvenile literature. 4. Nuclear fission—Juvenile literature. [1. Meitner, Lise, 1878-1968. 2. Physicists. 3. Scientists. 4. Women—Biography.] I. Title. II. Series.
    QC774.M4B36 2003
    539'.092—dc21   2003000347

ABOUT THE AUTHOR: Born in Boston, Massachussetts, **John Bankston** began publishing articles in newspapers and magazines while still a teenager. Since then, he has written over two hundred articles, and contributed chapters to books such as *Crimes of Passion,* and *Death Row 2000,* which have been sold in bookstores across the world. He has written more than three dozen biographies for young adults, including *Francis Crick and James Watson: Pioneers in DNA Research, Robert Goddard and the Liquid Rocket Engine,* and *Alexander Fleming and the Story of Penicillin* (Mitchell Lane). He has worked in Los Angeles, California as a producer, screenwriter and actor. Currently he is in pre-production on *Dancing at the Edge,* a semi-autobiographical screenplay he hopes to film in Portland, Oregon. Last year he completed his first young adult novel, *18 to Look Younger.* He currently lives in Portland, Oregon.

PUBLISHER'S NOTE: In selecting those persons to be profiled in this series, we first attempted to identify the most notable accomplishments of the 20th century in science, medicine, and technology. When we were done, we noted a serious deficiency in the inclusion of women. For the greater part of the 20th century science, medicine, and technology were male-dominated fields. In many cases, the contributions of women went unrecognized. Women have tried for years to be included in these areas, and in many cases, women worked side by side with men who took credit for their ideas and discoveries. Even as we move forward into the 21st century, we find women still sadly underrepresented. It is not an oversight, therefore, that we profiled mostly male achievers. Information simply does not exist to include a fair selection of women.

Contents

All Lise Meitner wanted was to become a scientist. In the early 1900s, that meant using a separate entrance to a laboratory, doing unpaid work, and being treated as though she were very different. She endured everything gracefully while pursuing her dreams.

Chapter 1

Barriers

The creation of the most destructive weapon the world has ever known began on a bleak December morning in 1938. A woman living in exile in Sweden left her hotel accompanied by her nephew, Otto Frisch. Both of them were scientists and they had a problem to solve.

They walked up and down in the snow. They talked rapidly, considering several ideas and then rejecting them. Gradually, though, the correct approach to the problem took shape. Finally they were satisfied that they had the solution.

It would soon change the world forever.

In that winter of 1938, Nazi Germany was arming for war. The nation's leader, Adolf Hitler, wanted to dominate the world. Soon he would become an enormous threat to the United States.

He was already a threat to the Jews, who were being rounded up and imprisoned. Because she had been born into a Jewish family, Frisch's aunt had escaped from Germany several months earlier. She was one of the lucky ones. By 1945, over six million Jews would be killed because of Hitler's policies. Yet the work she did with Frisch that night could have been of assistance to Hitler.

She certainly didn't want to help the Nazis. That December night all she wanted to do was solve a scientific riddle. She never imagined the deadly consequences of her answer. All she wanted to do, all she'd ever wanted to do, was be a scientist. She dreamed of conducting experiments and solving problems. But for women who grew up at the end of the nineteenth and early twentieth centuries, becoming a scientist was nearly an impossible dream.

All dreamers face obstacles. Many times those obstacles are created by others. Whether it's about changing the world or changing a life, dreams are often about change. This can scare people.

In 1905, patent clerk Albert Einstein had a "miracle year," a period when he published scientific papers examining the speed of light. At that time, few scientists understood his theories. They considered them to be impossible. It took years for these theories to be accepted. Yet today they form the cornerstone of modern physics.

Charles Drew was an African American who developed a revolutionary process to separate plasma, the liquid part of blood, from whole blood during the late 1930s. The plasma could then be frozen, which allowed it to be stored for an indefinite period of time. Before his discovery, donated blood had to be used within a week.

In 1941, Drew was appointed as director of the plasma storage program for the United States armed forces. He didn't stay long. The military demanded that he keep plasma donated by white people separate from what was donated by blacks. When he angrily responded that there wasn't a scientific basis for such a distinction, his superiors refused to budge. Drew resigned in disgust. It would be years before the military would acknowledge what Drew already knew—plasma is the same regardless of the donor's race, or even the donor's blood type.

In the 1940s, Dr. Jonas Salk applied to numerous medical foundations so he could study viruses. They turned him down. At least one foundation is believed to have rejected Salk because he was Jewish. Anti-Semitism—prejudice against Jews—was common in medicine. What he got instead was a job offer which would eventually lead him to develop the polio vaccine. That vaccine has saved countless lives.

This is the story of another dreamer who faced obstacles. As a woman she was expected to become a teacher, not a scientist. After she earned an advanced scientific degree, for several years she could only find work as an unpaid lab assistant. She was forced to work in a basement and use a separate entrance from the men.

Yet she never gave up. The work she eventually did has had an unimaginable impact on mankind. Her name is Lise Meitner, and her journey through the atomic age is the story of a dreamer who faced obstacles and overcame them.

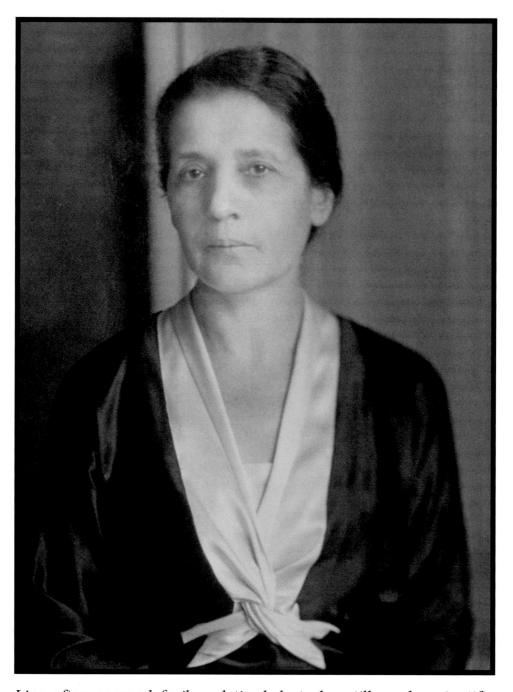

Lise often seemed frail and tired, but she still made scientific discoveries long before her male colleagues. First, though, she'd have to graduate from high school, which as a Jewish female was a challenge in itself.

Chapter 2

A Struggle to Learn

Elise Meitner was born in November, 1878. Although she'd celebrate her birthday on November 7, the birth register in Vienna listed it as November 17. Regardless, the girl they'd call "Lise" was born at 27 Kaiser Josefstrasse, in the apartment where her family lived in the Leopoldstadt district of Vienna. The city was the capital of Austria-Hungary, a loose collection of territories including Transylvania, Croatia and Bohemia along with the formerly separate countries of Austria and Hungary. It was an enormous and unruly empire.

Formerly a rundown Jewish ghetto, by the time of Lise's childhood her Vienna neighborhood was still segregated—only Jews lived there—but it was much nicer. Josefstrasse was lined with coffee shops and offices run by Jewish professionals. The street emptied into the enormous Prater Park, where the family regularly spent their Sundays together.

Her father, Philipp, had been one of the few Jewish men in Austria accepted to law school. He was descended from Jewish immigrants who'd come to Vienna in the late 1700s from the town of Meiethein in what is modern-day Czechoslovakia. They took the town's name and eventually shortened it to Meitner. Philipp's family had continually improved its lot in life, and he became a very successful attorney.

Lise's mother Hedwig, was the granddaughter of a Russian immigrant who'd fled that country's persecution of Jews. By the time Lise was born, her mother was already socially prominent. One of Hedwig's friends was the famous psychiatrist Sigmund Freud. Hedwig opened her home to the best and brightest in the Jewish community, not only preparing meals and drinks but also taking part in the conversations. The Meitner living room became a kind of Jewish salon, a place where discussions on art, politics, and Viennese society took place regularly. Hedwig was also a talented pianist who taught her children to play the instrument. Lise's hours in front of the keyboard gave her a love of music that remained throughout her life.

Though she was a shy girl, she was always eager to learn. Even from a young age, she showed a special interest in the natural world and a lively curiosity that's one of the marks of a good scientist.

"One day Lise noticed a beautiful, iridescent puddle of water with a bit of oil in it," says author Sharon Bertsch McGrayne in the book *Nobel Prize Women in Science.* "Why was the puddle filled with colors? she asked. The answer entranced her; she had not imagined that such marvelous things could be learned about nature. She became convinced that, if she worked hard enough, she could understand its laws."

With her deep thoughtful eyes and dark hair pulled tight against her high forehead, Lise could usually be found on the edges of the adults' conversations. Even as a child she was comfortable with these intelligent adults. She was always grateful to her parents for providing such an intellectually stimulating environment for their children.

The Meitner offspring were a large and occasionally unruly brood. In addition to Lise, there were her older sisters

Gisela and Auguste, two younger sisters and three younger brothers. They grew up in a time when the phrase "children should be seen and not heard" was on nearly every parent's lips. But Philipp and Hedwig weren't interested in being a traditional mother and father.

In fact, they weren't very interested in being traditional at all. Instead of embracing the Jewish religion, Philipp embraced law and politics, helping reform his country's constitution. Instead of putting his energy into being a practicing Jew, he devoted his time to his children. The Meitners didn't celebrate Passover (one of the major Jewish holidays) but they did celebrate every child's achievement.

Eventually several of their children would be baptized in Christian faiths, including Lise in 1908, abandoning their Jewish religion altogether. Of course anti-Semites—people who hate and try to oppress Jews—rarely care whether or not the Jews they're hurting are practicing.

For Lise and her siblings, their family's untraditional views meant one thing: opportunity! All the Meitner children were talented in one way or another. Auguste was a skilled composer and pianist, while other Meitners were sharp academically.

Of the eight children, Lise studied the hardest, often falling asleep with a math book tucked beneath her pillow. Whenever she didn't understand something, she would ask.

There was just one problem. At that time in Austria, girls weren't allowed to obtain a university education or even to attend secondary schools that would have challenged them intellectually. So Lise attended the Mädchen–Bürgerschule, a school for girls. She learned bookkeeping rather than mathematics, very basic science instead of chemistry, and mainly how to conduct herself as a proper young lady. The Mädchen–Bürgerschule was basically a preparatory academy—preparing its students for careers as wives and mothers.

Lise was 13 when she graduated. For most of her classmates, that was the end of their formal education. They would spend the next few years getting ready for marriage. But marriage had no appeal for Lise. Yet any education beyond the Mädchen–Bürgerschule meant just one thing: teacher training.

Of course, there's nothing wrong with becoming a teacher—if that's what a person *chooses* to do. Unfortunately, prior to the twentieth century, teaching was just about the only career option available to Austrian women. For Lise, it was like sitting down at a fancy restaurant and finding out you can only order the salad. She wanted to learn about science, not stand in front of young girls every day.

Despite her reluctance, Philipp convinced his daughter to become a French teacher. It would give her something to fall back on. Maybe one day there would be more options. So Lise bided her time at the Elevated High School for Girls and hoped for a better choice.

It took half a dozen years before opportunity arrived. University level education finally became available for women. One of the reasons was Austria-Hungary's occupation of Bosnia and Herzegovina, both of which had a large Muslim population. Since their religion would not allow a Muslim woman to be examined by a male doctor, Austria brought in female doctors from other countries. As the demand for female doctors grew, so too did the demands that Austria open her universities to women. In response the country's leaders began establishing gymnasiums (high schools) for women.

Unfortunately, by this time Lise was too old for high school. There was only one way for her to get accepted to the university. She'd have to pass the Matura, a test given when students completed gymnasium studies. Designed to examine them on their knowledge of subjects taught in high school, the test covered everything from advanced science courses like botany and zoology to classic languages like Greek and Latin.

Lise was going to have to take a test for material she'd never studied. Worse, she wouldn't just have to cover the courses she'd missed by not going to high school. She'd also have to make up for the poor education she got at the Mädchen-Bürgerschule.

There's an old saying that women have to do twice the work to get half the credit and if that was ever true, it was true of Lise Meitner. Ruth Lewis Simes's biography *Lise Meitner: A Life in Physics* quotes her as saying, "Thinking back to the time of my youth, one realizes with some astonishment how many problems then existed in the lives of ordinary young girls, which now seem almost unimaginable. Among the most difficult of these problems was the possibility of normal intellectual training."

There was only one way Lise would get "normal intellectual training." She'd have to study, study, study and then study some more. The other members of her family started making fun of her if she crossed the room without a book in her hand; she read just about *everywhere.* She had to, because it was the only way to cram what amounted to eight years worth of courses into as short a period of time as possible.

Lise managed to complete her studying in two years. Fortunately, she didn't have to do it alone. Along with two other young women, Lise began tutoring sessions in 1899 with Arthur Szarvassy. A young man with a fresh doctorate, he was unlike most teachers of the time because he treated the three women just as he would have treated men. He never let up on them and he never tried to "dumb down the material." Young Lise fell in love. Not with the tutor, but with physics. It was controversial, many scientists saw it as hocus-pocus, but Lise knew instinctively it was the science of the future.

Despite her love for the subject, Lise wasn't sure if she should pursue it as a career. It would have been an unstable profession for a man, let alone a woman. She wondered if maybe she should consider something safer, like medicine. Her father wouldn't hear of it. He encouraged her to pursue her dreams (although he also joked that only true geniuses should become doctors).

In July of 1901, Lise nervously walked into the Akademisches Gymnasium, a respected high school for boys from her neighborhood. In an unfamiliar school, tested by teachers she'd never met, the young woman was extremely nervous.

She didn't need to be. Fourteen women took the Matura that day. Only four passed. All three of Dr.

Szarvassy's young women qualified for college, and Lise was finally on her way. She was twenty-three years old and life's possibilities seemed as limitless as her imagination.

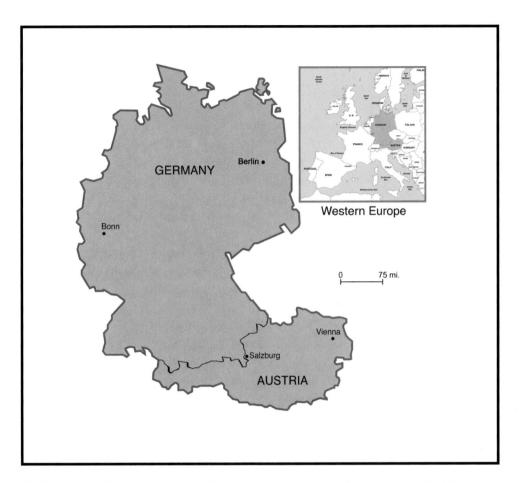

This map shows where Lise was born and grew up in Vienna, Austria. After she graduated from the University of Vienna, she could not find a job. So, in 1907, Lise went to Berlin to talk to Max Planck to see if she could attend his lectures. It was in Berlin that Lise met a young Dr. Otto Hahn.

Lise Meitner wasn't the only female scientist breaking down barriers in the early 1900s. Marie Curie's radioactive discoveries made her famous, but also cost her her life.

Chapter 3

A Radiation Education

People who courageously break down barriers are often seen as heroes and larger-than-life. It's important to remember that while their *deeds* are often heroic, these people are human beings, with the same fears and insecurities as anyone.

Lise Meitner didn't enter the University of Vienna standing tall as one of its few female students. She was terrified. Shy by nature, she became even more reclusive as she was surrounded by men. Worse, *these* men had finished high school. In spite of her high marks on the Matura, she worried that they would quickly pick up on her educational gaps. She compensated by studying twice as hard and speaking half as much—a pretty amazing accomplishment considering how studious and quiet she already was.

Lise's lack of confidence revealed itself in her second semester at the University. Her calculus professor asked her to find the mistake in a mathematician's work. Because her efforts were so involved and precise, he suggested that she should publish her work. But she felt that it would be wrong. That turned the professor against her.

Publishing a paper would have been a tremendous honor for a first-year student, but Lise didn't hesitate to turn it down. Then she decided to major in physics rather than mathematics. Again she had great luck with teachers. Sitting down in the classroom of Ludwig Boltzmann during her second year, Lise was immediately enthralled. Boltzmann was so enthusiastic about his subject that he carried his listeners along with him.

A burly man with a full beard and curly red hair, Boltzmann looked more like a lumberjack than a teacher. Despite his appearance, Boltzmann was unusually sensitive. Given to dark, brooding moods, the professor may have well been bipolar, a mental illness marked by days or weeks of high, frantic energy followed by periods of bleak despair. Lise knew little of this at the time, but she would later say it was Boltzmann's "humanity" which made him a great science teacher, particularly to one very shy and unsure young woman.

In the early 1900s, many fellow scientists questioned the validity of physics and Boltzmann's teaching of it. If the condition of the physics department of the University was any indication, the school wasn't too supportive either.

The lessons were conducted in a deteriorating apartment building. Purchased as a "temporary" home for the physics wing, it served as its location for nearly forty years. Its stairs were worn out and some of the floorboards were rotting. Lise was afraid that if a fire broke out it would be hard to escape.

In spite of the drab and dangerous conditions, Lise soon acquired another motivation beyond Boltzmann's teaching to continue her studies. A woman named Marie Curie was making her mark in nuclear physics, a discipline completely unheard of only a few years before. The study of atomic structure and the interaction of particles within the atom began with this former elementary school teacher in Poland during the 1890s.

Like Lise, Marie's parents valued education, and like Lise she struggled to get more than the typical education for a female. Although she was tutored at home, Marie eventually did attend a gymnasium—a rare thing for a young Polish woman in Warsaw in the 1880s.

Like Lise, she also couldn't immediately pursue higher education, having to tutor students and work as a governess. In the early 1890s, she was finally able to attend the Sorbonne, a very prestigious university in Paris. While she was there, she met fellow scientist Pierre Curie, and their marriage was about both romance and labor. Their discovery of the elements radium and polonium won them the Nobel Prize in physics in 1903. Though Pierre died in 1906, Marie devoted the rest of her life to the study of radioactivity, the emission of energy or particles from atoms that spontaneously break down. She won another Nobel Prize in 1911, this one in chemistry. Her work led to a variety of medical and scientific advances but also probably contributed to her death from leukemia in 1934.

The famous scientist Albert Einstein would later call Meitner "our Marie Curie," but what Lise embarked on would eventually alter the world in ways Marie Curie couldn't have imagined. Lise had long been fascinated by Marie Curie's research and began her own work with radioactivity shortly after earning her doctorate on February 1, 1906. She soon published an article in the scientific journal *Physikalische Zeitschrift* using just her first initial to conceal her gender.

Despite that achievement, Lise was miserable. She'd been the second woman in the University of Vienna's history to earn a doctorate in physics (Olga Steindler beat her by three years.). After getting her Ph.D. degree, Lise must have seen opportunity stretching before her like an uninterrupted dream.

The dream didn't last. No one wanted to hire a woman to teach physics. She did work far beneath her training, for no money. She was supported by a small allowance from her family and a teaching position at a local girls' school. Lise found the whole situation humiliating. All she could do was hope it wouldn't last forever.

It didn't. Sadly, Lise's job ended with tragedy. After battling depression for years, Dr. Boltzmann abruptly committed suicide. His loss devastated his young protégé; his encouragement of Lise had kept her going when few other things did.

That put her at a crossroads. It seemed that she had little to look forward to in Vienna. She felt she had to go somewhere else.

Then she met Max Planck, whose ideas about light and radiation known as quantum theory work would later earn him a Nobel Prize. The University was looking for a new physics professor to head up Dr. Boltzmann's department. Planck came to interview for Boltzmann's position. Although he quickly realized he wasn't interested in leaving a prestigious position in Berlin, Germany for such a poorly funded school, he did meet Lise. She nervously approached him and began discussing his work and her own interests in radiation. Some accounts suggest he invited her to attend the university in Berlin.

This wasn't very likely. In 1897, responding to the survey of a newspaper reporter, hundreds of learned men in Germany wrote about their views on women pursuing higher education. The views of Max Planck stood out even in this less enlightened time. While he admitted that in some extraordinary cases women should be admitted to college, he went on to write that "Amazons are abnormal, even in intellectual fields," referring to the legendary race of giant, war-like women. "Nature itself has designated for woman her vocation as mother and housewife."

Lise would become an exception to Planck's rule, but first she would have to go to Berlin. There was only one obstacle to this ambition: money. However, the shy young woman from Vienna was finally gaining a bit of confidence thanks to her Ph.D. and several complicated radioactivity experiments she'd conducted on her own. That gave her the courage to ask her parents to allow her to go to Berlin.

She was twenty-eight years old. Despite holding an advanced degree, she still needed an allowance from her parents just to get by. Yet somehow Lise knew Berlin would give her all the opportunities she could imagine. She just needed to convince the men in charge to get out of the way of her dreams.

Serious in this photograph, Otto Hahn could be jovial and light hearted, the perfect partner for studious Lise. His strength in chemistry balanced hers in physics and math.

Chapter 4
A Partnership Begins

When Dr. Lise Meitner arrived in Berlin in the fall of 1907, she was away from Austria for the first time and overwhelmed by the unfamiliar city. It was a place where monuments to wars won by Germany dominated the landscape—victories over countries like France, Denmark and Lise's own Austria-Hungary.

Yet as tough as the city may have seemed, it was nowhere near as difficult as the school. Founded in 1809 by Friedrich Wilhelm III, the Friedrich-Wilhelm Universtat was considered one of the finest colleges in all of Europe. It also didn't admit women. They were only allowed to audit classes—taking courses for no credit towards a degree. Lise was intimidated by the atmosphere at the school.

The first person Lise needed to talk to was Max Planck. She asked if she could attend his lectures. As she later remembered, Planck was cordial when he said, "But you are a doctor already. What more do you want?"

Lise wanted *everything*—the chance to learn from some of the best physicists in the world, the chance to use their laboratories. Most of all the chance to prove that her gender had nothing to do with her abilities. Instead, Lise quietly asked Planck if she could audit his classes.

Planck agreed. Although Lise's knowledge of advanced physics grew in Planck's classes, she still had plenty of free time to experiment. Soon she met another young scientist, Dr. Otto Hahn. Even though he was a few months younger, Hahn was a chemist who already had a strong reputation in radioactivity. He was looking for a physicist with whom he could collaborate on experiments. Lise was convinced he could teach her a great deal.

As things turned out, the two were perfect complements to each other. Hahn was a genius with chemistry, but lacked knowledge in physics or math. Lise was strong in math and physics but weaker in chemistry. Just as important for two people embarking on a partnership, their personalities meshed perfectly. Hahn's casual, light-hearted manner was balanced by Lise's studiousness. He brought her out of her shell, while she helped him focus more seriously.

However, Lise had to overcome the same types of barriers she'd been hurdling since adolescence before she could even begin. Hahn's laboratory was in the chemistry department. Since professors in Germany had near total control over the departments they ran, Lise first had to get permission from the department's head, Emil Fischer. Fischer generally barred women—he actually worried out loud that one of them might set her hair on fire (male hair was evidently inflammable.).

Lise was bold enough to ask permission, and Fischer eventually relented. There was one condition. Lise had to confine her experiments to the building's basement, a converted carpentry shop with its own separate entrance. Hahn helped her set it up as a radiation laboratory. But Lise couldn't go upstairs where Hahn's chemistry work was. In fact, whenever she needed to use a bathroom, she had to go outside and walk to a restaurant. It was a difficult situation, but Lise made the most of it.

Over the next several years Hahn and Lise conducted a number of experiments. They detailed their results in several articles in scientific journals; in every one Lise signed her name L. Meitner. One day a famous scientist named Ernest Rutherford visited their laboratory. Not only was he stunned to discover that Hahn's partner was a woman, he also paired her off with his wife. Hahn and Rutherford discussed experiments. Rather meekly, Lise went shopping with Rutherford's wife.

In the summer of 1912, Lise and Hahn moved into the spacious new Kaiser-Wilhelm Institute for Chemistry. Privately funded, it provided the best of equipment and a paying job for Hahn. Lise, despite five years of collaboration, got nothing better than the right to work there as Hahn's "guest."

Lise was in her thirties and she was still working for free. Her situation only grew more difficult following her father's death in 1910. Surprisingly, Max Planck helped her out. He appointed her to be his "assistent," which made her the first woman "assistent" in the entire country. A woman who had published several important scientific papers was earning her living by grading students' papers. Though it was still her first paying position, it didn't provide her with much money. She became accustomed to a diet of black bread and coffee. Soon afterward, the University of Prague (in Czechoslovakia) offered her an assistant professorship. The Kaiser Wilhelm Institute decided that she was too valuable to lose and offered her a salary.

Even as Lise's academic career blossomed, the outside world intruded. Various ethnic groups inside the Austria-Hungarian empire had been raging over ancient tensions for years, but in 1914 their anger boiled over.

In the beginning, Max Planck had advanced views on physics but traditional views on a woman's role. He doubted women could ever be successful in science. Lise Meitner quickly proved him wrong.

Chapter 5
Conflict

The seed of what was called the Great War (it would later be known as World War I) sprouted on June 28, 1914. The heir to the Austria-Hungarian throne, the Archduke Franz Ferdinand, was assassinated in Sarajevo, Serbia. Supported by Germany, Austria-Hungary sent an ultimatum to Serbia. The response was hostile.

Austria-Hungary declared war. The Serbs were allied with Russia, and Russian troops mobilized against the Austrian border. In the following weeks, countries who held treaties with the opposing countries were dragged into the conflict. Across the ocean, the United States and Canada would eventually be summoned as well.

Living in Berlin as the war began, Lise was able to witness firsthand Germany's preparation for war and the overwhelming support it received from the population. Every day, Lise watched as soldiers boarded trains bound for the front lines. Otto Hahn was among them. He enlisted as a soldier, but he was quickly recruited for his scientific training. He was one of an elite group of German scientists working to perfect chemical weapons. From chlorine to mustard gases, the chemicals were horrific and deadly. Those who survived were often permanently disabled.

Unable to be a soldier, or participate as a similarly trained male might have, Lise became a nurse, studying anatomy and how to perform x-rays. While taking her classes, she continued some experiments which she'd begun with Hahn and also began another series of experiments on her own. But soon her work was interrupted.

In June of 1915, Lise boarded a train for Vienna. After a brief stop, she headed toward Russia. Arriving at a military hospital forty-miles from the front lines, she was unprepared for the sheer numbers of wounded and the degree of their suffering. Besides using the x-ray machine, she also assisted the doctors with amputations. This was nasty and frequent work because infections were larger problems on those battlefields than they are today.

In 1916, the battles near where Lise was based slowed down. She received a transfer. Before reaching her assignment, she had time to work at Vienna's Radium Institute. Around this time she turned down a marriage proposal from a Greek professor. It's the only known proposal she received.

There was little room in Lise's life for marriage. In fact there was little room for the war. When she reached her new assignment in Poland, she found the doctors sick and tired, scarcely able to take care of themselves, let alone the wounded. She felt useless and unnecessary, and hoped that she could go back to the Kaiser Wilhelm Institute.

She was soon given permission to do just that. Returning to Berlin, Lise found her familiar environment altered by the war effort, turned into labs for chemical weapons and the like. However, the war gave Lise one advantage. Most of the men were still fighting and in 1917 she was put in charge of organizing the physical radioactivity department. Although Hahn would be able to get released from his duties from time to time, for the first time Lise was in charge overseeing assistants and students.

She already knew that whenever uranium was found in minerals, the element actium was found as well. Many scientists believed that uranium decayed into actium. But if that was the case, there was probably an element in between the two. Just as her idol Marie Curie worked to isolate radium, Lise began searching for this intermediate element. Working with Hahn whenever he could get leave, she tried to discover this element.

In January of 1918, she succeeded. Excitedly she wrote Hahn the good news. A short time later the two wrote a scientific paper calling the new element protactinium. With an abbreviation of Pa, it would become the ninety-first element on the Periodic Table of the Elements. Although Hahn was gone most of the time and Lise did the majority of the research, she still allowed his name to appear as "senior author" on the paper they submitted. This would suggest that he'd supervised all of the experiments. Lise would later pay a heavy price for her generosity.

However, her focus turned to greater matters by the fall of 1918. On November 11, an armistice or treaty was signed. The conflict then called "The War to End All Wars" was over. For Lise Meitner and the rest of Germany the pain was just beginning.

Once a failed painter and jailed revolutionary, Adolf Hitler eventually gained enough support that the German President Paul von Hindenburg allowed him to form a new government. Soon the dictator's policies would threaten Lise's dreams.

Chapter 6
Fission

The so-called "War to End all Wars" ended nothing but lives, millions of them. It also began the resentment and anger that led to an even more destructive war in just over two decades. The conditions forced upon Germany by the Treaty of Versailles left the country broke and humiliated, its people starving and angry. Prices rose to incredible levels. Not far from the Kaiser Wilhelm Institute, a failed painter named Adolf Hitler was about to change Lise's life forever.

In 1923, he tried to overthrow the German government. After nine months in jail, Hitler began gaining popularity and power. His Nazi party was anti-Semitic and by the late 1920s some Jews began fleeing from Germany. They chose poverty in exile over the life they feared they'd have in Nazi Germany.

Despite the ominous political developments in the background, Lise's career continued to advance. She'd been appointed director of the physics section of the Kaiser Wilhelm Institute's Chemistry Section in 1919. She was also appointed assistant professor, the first woman to achieve that level. Seven years later she became a full professor at the University of Berlin, the first woman to rise that high.

By now, Lise and Hahn rarely worked together. She was no longer in his shadow and was probably better known that he was. She was accepted on an equal footing with the great physicists of that era, several of whom would become Nobel Prize winners. She was even considered several times for that honor herself.

Meanwhile the Nazi Party was gaining power. Hitler found support among the German people by pledging a return of the national pride lost after World War I. Many of the speeches that Hitler and other members of his party gave blamed their country's problems on the Jewish middle class, which they claimed controlled banking and commerce.

In 1933, German President Paul von Hindenburg gave Adolf Hitler the authority to form a new government. Hitler soon eliminated free speech. Most who opposed him in his quest for power were quickly imprisoned and even killed. Hitler's "Final Solution" called for the eventual extermination, or elimination, of people such as Jews and Gypsies. These people were restricted in their movement and regularly assaulted by Nazi supporters.

Hahn returned from a trip to the United States to find that the Kaiser Wilhelm Institute's director had resigned. Hahn took his place. He was forced to fly the Nazi swastika flag and pledge his loyalty to the party.

Lise was banned from teaching, but she could continue to do research. Although she was angry that so many now seemed to see her Jewish background as negatively as they'd once viewed her gender, Lise refused to give up. She knew in her heart that the atomic age was cresting. The wave of opportunity was about to crash into her front door.

Several decades of research had given physicists a much better understanding of the atom. They knew that atoms aren't solid particles. They are mainly empty space. Most of the atom's mass is in its central core, or nucleus, which consists of two different particles—protons and neutrons. Whirling quickly around the nucleus, like planets in an orbit around the sun, are electrons. Protons have a positive electric charge and electrons a balancing negative charge. Neutrons, discovered in 1932 by James Chadwick, were electrically neutral.

Increasingly, attention was being focused on the nucleus. Early in 1934, Marie Curie's daughter Irene and her husband Frederic Joliot caused an atom to give off radiation by bombarding its nucleus with charged particles. As the couple explained in a statement to the press, "For the first time it is possible to produce by exterior cause the radioactivity of certain atomic nuclei."

The couple's breakthrough inspired an Italian scientist named Enrico Fermi. He believed that an electrically neutral particle—the neutron—would produce better results.

Fermi's group bombarded the first 91 elements, using neutrons as the "bullets." Then they reached uranium. With an atomic number of 92, it was the heaviest known natural element. Fermi believed that its nucleus, or center, would absorb the neutrons. That would produce even heavier, man-made elements called "transuranic elements."

However, his experiments generated so much radioactivity that it was virtually impossible to identify any elements. It didn't matter. Believing that Fermi had discovered new elements, other physicists raced to their labs to join the hunt for still others. Lise wanted to get involved in this process. She asked Hahn to join her because she needed an expert chemist to help identify the tiny samples that the experiments produced. They were joined by Fritz Strassman, a young chemist who worked with Hahn. For four years, they didn't accomplish very much. Neither did any of the other researchers.

In the meantime, powerful political forces were at work. In March, 1938, Hitler's forces crossed the border into Austria and annexed it. Even the Nazis were shocked by the way many Viennese attacked their Jewish neighbors. Jews were beaten and even murdered in the streets. Some committed suicide to escape the brutality. Lise realized immediately how much danger she was in. She could no longer rely on her Austrian citizenship to protect her in Germany. Hahn even told her not to come to the Institute anymore.

In May, Lise began to craft an escape plan. She turned to Sweden even as the Nazi government refused her request for a passport. It was "considered undesirable that well-known Jews leave Germany," the unwelcome letter from the Ministry of the Interior informed her. It didn't matter that she'd converted to Protestantism three decades earlier. To the Nazis, it was a case of once a Jew, always a Jew.

She'd have to sneak out. If she was caught, she could be thrown into a concentration camp or even executed. Aided by friends, Lise pulled together some money and the promise of a job at Sweden's Research Institute for Physics. On July 13, she boarded a train in Berlin. Hahn gave his grandmother's diamond ring to her in case she needed to bribe border officials. Despite her fears, Lise crossed the border without incident. Once in Sweden she began corresponding regularly with her partner as he continued their experiments.

Later that year, Hahn and Strassman thought they'd "chipped away" part of the uranium nucleus and produced radium. However, radium is separated by four atomic numbers from uranium. At that time, no one believed that such a drastic change could occur.

Lise certainly didn't. In November that year, she and Hahn met secretly in Copenhagen, Denmark. She chided her partner for his results, calling them a "nightmare" and "nonsense." She urged him to examine what he and Strassman were doing much more closely.

A month later, Hahn realized that what he had thought was radium was actually barium. The two substances are very similar chemically. That presented an even greater puzzle. Barium's atomic number was 56. That was just over half of the original uranium nucleus. There was nothing in the laws of physics that could explain such a radical change. Even if that could happen, what happened to the rest of the nucleus? It couldn't just disappear.

That was when Lise and her nephew had their walk in the Swedish winter snow.

If Hahn had been any other scientist, she would have assumed he'd made a mistake. But Meitner knew him. She'd worked with him.

After she'd analyzed the problem with her nephew for some time, Lise had a sudden flash of insight. She compared the nucleus of a uranium atom to a drop of water or a balloon filled with water. It was already a little unstable because of the strong electrical current of its 92 protons. When an incoming neutron struck the nucleus with a great deal of force, it would begin to wobble and form two bulges with a narrow neck connecting them. Then the neck would snap and two new nuclei would be created. While in theory they could be almost anything, barium (atomic number 56) and krypton (36) were the most common.

She realized that Hahn's experiment hadn't just chipped at the nucleus of the uranium. He'd split it nearly in half! Atoms could be divided, even changed. When that happened, an enormous energy release would occur because each of the two new nuclei had a positive charge and would repel each other. She carefully calculated this potential energy release, relying in part on Einstein's theory of relativity. Despite its complexity, this very elegant, and simple looking equation is probably the most famous formula in history: $e = mc^2$.

In this formula, e is energy, m is mass and c is the speed of light. Einstein's formula showed that matter—or mass—is really solidified energy. It only takes a relatively small amount of matter to release a tremendous amount of energy. This formula explains how our sun has been able to produce heat and light for billions of years.

When Lise finished her calculations, she was astonished. She checked them again.

She'd proved it. A single gram of uranium, under the right conditions, could release as much energy as many pounds of dynamite. Hahn's discovery could lead to a weapon of unimaginable consequence.

Hahn hadn't done anything new. Irene Curie, Frederic Joliet, Enrico Fermi, even Hahn himself had actually been splitting the atom for four years during their experiments. They just hadn't realized it, because they had been looking for larger, transuranium atoms. It was Lise's genius to demonstrate that they should have been looking in the other direction.

Hahn referred to the process as "bursting." Lise and her nephew wanted a better term. In nature, when a cell splits apart it is called "fission." So they called this splitting of the atom "nuclear fission."

Frisch repeated Hahn's experiment, checking for the energy release. He realized that during the bombardment the fission released several stray neutrons. These neutrons could then bombard and split other uranium neutrons, which in turn could yield even more neutrons. This process would continue until, at a certain point, it would explode with tremendous force. It soon became known as a chain reaction.

Lise's first reaction to Hahn's experiment was typically modest. She sent Hahn a letter congratulating him on his work. She told him that "I am happy for the wonder of these findings," according to *Nobel Prize Women in Science.*

Yet the woman who had to use her own inferior laboratory three decades earlier had out-thought everyone else connected with one of the most important discoveries of the twentieth century.

One of them was the eminent Danish physicist Niels Bohr, who won the Nobel Prize in 1922. Frisch quickly told him about his aunt's explanation.

Bohr smacked himself on the forehead. "Oh, what idiots we have all been," he exclaimed.

Lise may have seen the wonder in Hahn's work. Others saw much more sinister uses for it. Einstein and other prominent scientists quickly realized the implications. They knew that it could lead to the construction of bombs of indescribable power. Einstein wrote a letter to U.S. President Franklin Roosevelt in August, 1939, explaining the danger if Hitler was the first to develop such bombs.

Within a month, any remaining questions about Germany's intentions were answered. In a surprise invasion, the German army swept into Poland. Outnumbered and unprepared, the Poles were quickly defeated. World War II had begun. Even though the United States wasn't officially at war, Roosevelt recognized the threat created by Nazi Germany. That threat intensified the following year when Germany conquered Norway. The country contained a factory that produced so-called "heavy water," another vital element in producing atomic weapons.

When the United States entered the war following a surprise attack on Pearl Harbor by Germany's ally Japan on December 7, 1941, Roosevelt had already begun the effort to design an atomic bomb. Code-named the "Manhattan Project," the effort would cost over two billion dollars in less than four years. This was an enormous amount of money sixty years ago, more than the value of the entire automotive industry. The Manhattan Project consisted of several separate laboratories working toward a common goal: building an atomic bomb. In 1943, a group of British scientists prepared to go to Los Alamos, New Mexico where much of the work was taking place. Lise was asked to join them. According to several scientists, Lise angrily replied, "I will have nothing to do with a bomb!"

She had imagined wonderful uses for nuclear fission. She was shocked by the idea that it might be used to kill people. Yet as worried as she was by American efforts, Lise was far more nervous about Germany's plans.

As things turned out, she had little reason to worry. Despite their advantages, the Nazis never came close to constructing an atomic bomb. One important reason was the many talented Jewish scientists who'd fled Hitler's oppression. Many became part of the Manhattan Project. In addition, Hitler never seemed to fully grasp the awesome destructive power of atomic energy. He occasionally referred to nuclear physics as "Jewish physics."

In 1944, Otto Hahn won the Nobel Prize for Chemistry for his role in the discovery of nuclear fission. Lise received no recognition. Many people consider this omission one of the most shameful oversights in Nobel prize history.

Germany surrendered in May, 1945. Two months later, the first successful test of an atomic bomb took place. It was an awesome sight. A mushroom-shaped cloud blasted 40,000 feet over the desert sky and blinding light flashed below while the ground shook violently. The bomb was a success—that single blast was equivalent to more than 20,000 tons of dynamite.

On August 6, 1945, a U.S. B-29 heavy bomber nicknamed the "Enola Gay" after the pilot's mother dropped an atomic weapon on the city of Hiroshima. The destructive power of that bomb, and the one which followed it at Nagasaki three days later, vaporized buildings and killed over 150,000 people in a single blast of heat and light. Just as many would die later from illnesses caused by radiation.

Lise was relaxing at a Swedish resort when she learned the news. A reporter seeking her opinion woke her with a phone call. Stunned, Lise spent the next few hours aimlessly wandering in the nearby woods. When she returned to her hotel, she found a pile of messages from news organizations.

Everyone wanted to interview the woman who'd helped to split the atom and then fled the Nazis.

Many even thought she'd secretly given all the bomb-making information to the Americans. But Lise had not been part of the atomic bomb program, and she felt the physics involved was beyond anything she was familiar with. Still, she'd helped to start it all. And that knowledge haunted her.

Three days later, Lise participated in a trans-Atlantic radio interview with President Roosevelt's widow, Eleanor. Lise would complain that the interview went poorly. Later that year, she was elected as a foreign member of the Swedish Academy of Science, one of only three women so honored in two centuries.

Early the following year, she traveled to the United States to visit family members and friends. She also taught a semester at the Catholic University of America in Washington, D.C. She was so well-known that MGM studios wanted to make a movie that featured her contributions to the making of the atomic bomb. She refused, even though she was offered a great deal of money.

In 1947, Strassman invited her to return to Germany and become director of the Kaiser Wilhelm Institute, which had now been renamed to honor Max Planck. Again she refused. She didn't believe that the German people fully realized the atrocities that had been committed in their name.

She continued to work, primarily in Sweden, until 1960. Then she retired and moved to Cambridge, England, where several of her relatives lived. In 1966, she shared the

Enrico Fermi Award with Hahn and Strassman. Unfortunately, by then she was too ill to attend the ceremony.

Lise Meitner died on October 27, 1968.

Ten years later, her native country of Austria produced a postage stamp on the occasion of the 100th anniversary of her birth.

In 1982, German physicists fused isotopes of bismuth and iron to create element 109. It became the heaviest known element on earth. A decade later, it was named Meitnerium in Lise's honor. With the symbol Mt, it serves as a permanent memorial to her life and work.

"Lise Meitner should be honored for her fundamental work on the physical understanding of fission," said Peter Armbruster, the physicist in charge of the research, as quoted in *Nobel Prize Women in Science*. "She should be honored as the most significant woman scientist of this century."

Despite her shyness, Lise would probably have been flattered. She may also have wanted to leave behind another legacy as well.

Although she'd never cared for the broadcast she made with Eleanor Roosevelt in 1945, the words she spoke on that occasion still have meaning today.

"Women have a great responsibility," she said, "and they are obliged to try, so far as they can, to prevent another war."

Lise Meitner Chronology

1878 Born in Vienna, Austria on either November 7 or 17

1892 Graduates from Mädchen-Bürgerschule (elementary and junior high school for girls)

1899 Begins studying for Matura (University admissions test)

1901 Passes Matura; enters University of Vienna

1906 Receives Ph.D. degree in physics

1907 Begins studying at the Friedrich-Wilhelm Universtat in Berlin; meets Otto Hahn

1912 Joins Kaiser Wilhelm Institute in Berlin; Max Planck provides her first paying job

1915 Works as nurse during World War I

1917 Discovers protactinium, element 91 on the Periodic Table of the Elements

1919 Becomes head of physics department at Kaiser Wilhelm Institute

1926 Is appointed professor of physics at the University of Berlin

1934 Begins studying the effects of bombarding uranium nuclei with neutrons with Hahn and Fritz Strassman

1938 Flees Germany for Sweden; realizes that experiments with uranium have split the atom

1939 Along with nephew Otto Frisch, applies term "nuclear fission" to process of splitting the atom

1943 Refuses to participate in Manhattan Project to build atomic bomb

1945 Elected to Swedish Royal Academy of Sciences

1946 Visits United States and teaches briefly at Catholic University of America in Washington, D.C.

1949 Wins Max Planck Medal

1960 Moves to Cambridge, England

1966 Wins Enrico Fermi Prize with Hahn and Strassman

1968 Dies on October 27

1978 Appears on Austrian postage stamp in honor of 100th anniversary of her birth

Nuclear Timeline

400 BC	The Greek philosopher Democritus gives name of "atomos" to the tiniest particles of matter.
1808	English chemist John Dalton publishes his theories on atoms.
1860s	Russian scientist Dmitri Mendeleyev develops the Periodic Table of the Elements.
1866	Alfred Nobel invents dynamite.
1895	Wilhelm Roentgen discovers X-rays.
1896	Henri Becquerel discovers uranium's radioactivity.
1897	Joseph John Thompson discovers electrons.
1898	Marie and Pierre Curie discover radium.
1900	Max Planck develops his quantum theory.
1905	Albert Einstein publishes the theory of relativity.
1908	Ernest Rutherford and Hans Geiger invent radiation counter
1919	Rutherford discovers the proton.
1932	James Chadwick proves existence of neutron.
1934	Irene Joliot-Curie and Frederic Joliet bombard nuclei of uranium atoms with alpha particles.
1938	Otto Hahn and Fritz Strassman split nucleus of a uranium atom.
1939	World War II begins; Lise Meitner and Otto Frisch coin the term "nuclear fission" and calculate enormous energy release.
1942	The first chain reaction nuclear reactor is successfully tested in Chicago.
1945	Atomic bombs are dropped on Japanese cities of Hiroshima and Nagasaki; World War II ends.
1949	The Soviet Union successfully tests an atomic bomb.
1952	A hydrogen bomb is tested for the first time.
1954	The world's first nuclear power plant opens near Moscow.
1957	The first nuclear power plant in the United States, located near Shippingport, Pennsylvania, begins producing electricity.
1960	The U.S. nuclear-powered submarine *Triton* circles the world while entirely submerged.
1979	The U.S. nuclear power plant at Three Mile Island, Pennsylvania, has a partial meltdown.
1982	German scientists produce element 109, which is later given the name of Meitnerium.
1986	Accident at the Soviet nuclear plant in Chernobyl
1996	The United Nations adopts a nuclear test ban treaty.
2003	U.S. Navy turns its base on the island of Vieques over to the Department of the Interior, ending 60 years of military testing there. Among the toxic pollutants left behind are depleted uranium shells.

Further Reading

For Young Adults

Barron, Rachel Stiffler. *Lise Meitner: Discoverer of Nuclear Fission.* Greensboro, N.C.: Morgan Reynolds, Inc. 2000.

Berger, Melvin. *Atoms, Molecules and Quarks.* New York: G.P. Putnam and Sons, 1986.

Henderson, Harry. *Nuclear Physics.* New York: Facts on File, Inc., 1998.

Stein, Conrad R. *Austria: Enchantment of the World.* New York: Grolier, 2000.

Stille, Darlene. *Extraordinary Women Scientists* Chicago: Children's Press, 1995.

Works Consulted

Boorse, Henry A., Lloyd Moltz, and Jefferson Hane Weaver. *The Atomic Scientists: A Biographical History.* New York: John Wiley, 1989.

McGrayne, Sharon Bertsch. *Nobel Prize Women in Science.* New York: Birch Lane Press, 1993.

Moore, Ruth. *Niels Bohr: The Man, His Science and the World They Changed.* Cambridge, MA: MIT Press, 1985.

Rhodes, Richard. *The Making of the Atom Bomb.* New York: Simon and Schuster, 1986.

Rhodes, Richard. *Dark Sun: The Making of the Hydrogen Bomb.* New York: Simon and Schuster, 1995.

Sime, Ruth Lewin. *Lise Meitner: A Life in Physics.* Berkeley, CA: University of Califorinia Press, 1996.

On the Internet

http://www.rhhct.org.uk/news/rhhct17/17.html

http://www.users.bigpond.com/Sinclair/fission/LiseMeitner.html

http://homepage.mac.com/dtrapp/people/Meitnerium.html

http://www.energyquest.ca.gov/scientists/meitner.html

Glossary

atom - smallest unit which makes up a chemical element

chain reaction - neutrons from one atomic fission trigger more fissions, releasing still more neutrons

electron - tiny, negatively charged particle that is part of an atom

element - basic substance which cannot be broken down into simpler substances

exile - living in another country, either from choice or from being forced to leave

fission - breakdown of atoms structure "splitting the atom" because atom is "split" into two nuclei

iridescent - producing a display of several different colors

isotopes - two or more atoms of a chemical element with the same atomic number but different mass and different behavior (such as uranium 235 and 238)

molecule- combinations of different atoms, such as water

nucleus - center of the atom

neutron - uncharged particle the size of a proton that is found in the nucleus of an atom

Periodic Table of the Elements - an arrangement of the elements based on their atomic numbers and relationships with each other.

physics - study of matter and energy and the relationships between them

plasma - liquid portion of blood

protégé - someone whose training or career is assisted by a more influential person

proton - positively charged particle found in atom's nucleus

radioactivity - energy or particles sent out from atoms that spontaneously break down

reactor - device that uses controlled nuclear fission to create power or radioactive substances

Index